WON MY MARRIAGE BACK

Copyright

Copyright © 2016
Publication> by <Stephonia Bush All rights reserved.

This book or any portion thereof may not be reproduced or used in any manner whatsoever without the express written permission of the publisher except for the use of brief quotations in a book review or scholarly journal.

First Printing: 2016
Publisher: Stephonia Bush

UNITED STATES

ISBN: 978-0-578-19012-9

About the Author

Stephonia Bush is the dedicated wife of Charley Bush and mother of Jahmil, Yontrey, & Zyah. My story is really very simple – I Love the Lord Jesus Christ. My passion is to spread the good news of God's love and restoration power in marriage and family. I am grateful for a God that loves me enough to give His life for me. I am thankful for a God that saw the mess that I was and put a plan of redemption in place just for me. I am honored that God thought I was worth saving.

I Love You Jesus!!

Dedications:

God- First and Foremost.

Thank You Most Gracious and Loving Father for entrusting me with this talent. May I be the servant you had in mind. I want to be everything you saw when you purposed me. I can do All things. In You.

My Husband Charley

Where would I be if it wasn't for you love. You are my rock. Thank you for loving a difficult me. This journey with you has been worth everything we are. Thank You for being giving of our time. Thank you for your never-ending support. I Love You with a love I can't explain. I promise you the day AFTER forever.

To My Children Jahmil, Yontrey, Zyah

You never doubted me. Your trust in me is unwavering. You three are my greatest inspiration. WE MADE IT!!

To My God Daughter Deja

Your strength and endurance help push me. You fought through a lot and won. You inspired me to keep pressing.

To My Pastors
Bishop Clarke & Prophetess Diane Lazare

The amount of leadership you poured into me is immeasurable. Thank you for your wisdom words. Thank you for being that example of God's love active in marriage. I followed you. And you took me somewhere.

Last, but not Least

To my parents and family

Thank you for being a part of my world. Because of you, I am rich. God placed me in a family of greatness. How can I not be great? We rise together. And we're on the move, Again

Table of Contents

Chapter One: What Is Marriage

Chapter Two: Our Story

Chapter Three: Becoming One

Chapter Four: Inviting God In

Chapter Five: Becoming The Wife God Had In Mind

Chapter 1: What Is Marriage

Physical marriage is legally entering into an agreement to live as man and wife. It is a natural and worldly commitment to join together in the state of matrimony.

Marriage is a proclamation of your intent to live together through good and bad situations and love each other through all circumstances. This is the only partnership that requires total commitment of all your resources. Marriage vows promise commitment for better or worse, for richer or poorer, in sickness and in health, making it top priority until death. Marriage is a daily commitment of your time, attention, finances, health and well-being. And the expectation is that this commitment lasts forever. This oath is taken in the presence of required witnesses, and the municipal authority stamp that certificate, the world expects you to become one unit. People expect you to speak in the terms of this partnership. Husband and wife now become members of the most prestigious merger that can be accomplished. They are thought to be embarking on the easiest, hardest, most trying, most fulfilling, longest, and most rewarding journey of their lives. There is no journey like the marriage journey.

Spiritually, marriage is the joining together of a man and a woman in covenant with God, to give of one's whole self-unto the other. It is agreeing to become one - mind, body, and spirit in the presence of the Lord. It is the place where two kindred spirits reunite in the divine purpose of their creation. When a man and a women decide to take the physical vows, their spirits are making the same proclamation of commitment to the heavens. The vows are the same better, worse, richer, poorer, sickness, health, unto death. God requires the same commitment in spiritual marriage. In this spiritual commitment, the husband's purpose reunites with his wife's purpose. It's like putting a puzzle back together. Every part of him fits effortlessly with every part of her. God's expectations are the same. The couple is required to operate within the realms of this partnership. However, there is one difference between physical and spiritual marriage. In the natural when two people join together in marriage, the world sees two people joining together to operate as one unit. In the spirit, the two spirits is seen as one. This joining would be equivalent to two people physically sharing the same body. In the spirit, you become one voice, one movement, one plan, one being.

Marriage is a partnership. Wikipedia defines a partnership as an arrangement where parties, known as partners. agree to cooperate to advance their mutual interest. The parties in this partnership is husband and wife. The mutual interest should be the marriage. In order for the partnership to work, both parties must "agree to cooperate". This cooperation requires that both parties have the same goal. The parties involved must confidently want the same successful outcome. This doesn't mean the parties will instantly or readily agree on the methods to achieve this goal. You will definitely differ in methods sometimes due to you both being born to separate people, raised in separate families, and having separate life experiences. In a merger, both parties keep the best of their company in an effort to make a better company. There are no one size fits all methods to achieve the goal. Neither parties will have all the answers needed to achieve the objective. Success will take agreement and compromise. Marriage is no different from any other successful merger in that it requires partnership to be successful. The parties in this merger is the husband and wife. Methods can be worked out on the journey to fulfillment of the objective. Remember, a successful marriage is the most rewarding merger you will ever enter into. And it is the only one that is designed, governed, and purposed by God To Last FOREVER.

Chapter 2: OUR STORY

Let's travel back through our life for a bit. When we met, both of us were very sexually active without the requirement of commitment. Yes, we were a little loose. Our stories were very much the same. He had just separated from his wife. And I was committed to a man that wasn't all the way committed to me. We both had thrown ourselves into this single lifestyle determined to make it work. We worked for the same company and was looking for the next escapade. We were introduced by a fellow co-worker. Our connection was instant. We literally talked all night. I we seem so much alike. He understood me without explanation. And I got him. It was like we had met and talked in a previous life. It was already so refreshing just to talk to him. I was definitely intrigued by this stranger soulmate. After a few phone conversations, we decided to meet in person. Individually, we had the same purpose, plan, and goal for initial meetings with the opposite sex. The goal was to have sex. So needless to say, our first meeting was set up with the intent to sleep together. I call it a meeting because SEX was the goal. We met up, had lunch first and talked. There was automatic chemistry. We had a lot in common. We grew up in the same city. We hung out in the same neighborhoods. Most of our families knew each other. We were both former believers in God. And we were previously dedicated and faithfully servers in church. Both having left the church; we secretly missed our fellowship with God and longed for that relationship back. Our lunch date lasted for hours. We laughed and talked as if we were catching up on old times. This chemistry would make having sex that much more enjoyable. One-night stands were our specialty. But the way our chemistry was set up, we could become sex buddies. After we had lunch, we went back to his place. This is how most of our relationships started. Sex became the standard by which our relationship's longevity was determined. To our surprise, nothing happened. There was a powerful attraction between us that went beyond the sexual. We had connected on a level we could not readily explain. Both of us were used to sex on the first date. Both of us was used to being the initiator of sex. Both of us had an overwhelming desire to have sex with each other. But neither of us could find the courage to start something. For the first time, we were waiting on the other person to start. There was something intriguing about each of us that peaked the other one's interest. Because sex was the goal, I was still trying to give the goodies away. He decided that we should wait. So, we dated. We were extremely comfortable with each other. We really understood each other.

I could just talk to him without having to explain myself first. Our minds thought on the same patterns. We wanted the same things out of life. And we wanted to share world. I will have to admit that not having sex was uncomfortable for me. This request from him to wait was really messing with my mind. I never waited for sex. Sex was how I said, "I like you." But we were waiting. I played along with the waiting game. But I made sure he knew that sex was available – at a moment's notice. Three weeks went by and still no sex. Four week later and we still had not done anything. Usually I would have lost interest, but this guy was different. The longer he made me wait the more attractive he became. I was used to getting what I wanted from men. He was willfully resisting me. It was driving me crazy. The longer I waited the harder I tried to give the goodies away. The harder I tried, the longer he made me wait. After a couple of weeks, I was in love. He was everything I wanted. This man fit into my world like he grew up there. He knew what made me smile. He knew what made me sad. I could trust him with everything me. Before him, my grandmother was the only person I ever trusted with me. But I trusted him. And just when I though he could not be more perfect, my son decided to call him daddy. And he was okay with it. My nieces and nephews adored him. My family welcomed him. His family did not care for me at first, but that's another book. We waited six weeks before we had sex. We were in deep like with each other. He was the first person I thought about when I got up. We spent weeks of late-night breathing on the phone not wanting to hang up first. Romantic walks on the beach filled our nights. Plans of a long life together began. For the first time in a long time, we only wanted one person - each other. Our prayers had been answered in each other. Finally, we had found a replica of God's love.

Pause!!! Heed my warning, "There is no replica of God's love. You will never find it in man (or woman).

Convinced that we had found "the one" after a month - we moved in together.

Our happily ever after had begun. Life together was good. We got along beautifully. It was a happy house. Marriage was the next obvious step. A relationship this perfect should end up in marriage. And Soon!!

It Resembled Real Marriage

Household responsibilities, my (our) son, and family decisions, we made together. Our joint life was stamped with joint bank accounts, shared bills, trips to the grocery store, road trips, and family reunions.

It's beginning to look a lot like family. When two people fall in love, moved in together and begin building a life together, the only thing left to do is reproduce their love. Two months into sharing the same address, we decided to have a baby. This joining of our love would be his first baby. I had wanted another baby since my son was two. I became a single mother with him and didn't want to have another baby alone. I wanted to find the right father before I had another baby. Finally, I found him. He was super excited about having a baby. Two months later we got pregnant. The next nine months was an emotional roller coaster mainly because I was pregnant. My first pregnancy I endured alone. This time I had help. This man was a wonderful pregnancy partner. He was catering and loving. He allowed me to quit my job. He took great care of me. As we approached our one-year anniversary as a couple, we were preparing for our son to be born the next month. Settling into the image of our future together, we got engaged. Our fairytale love had finally come to fruition. I was convinced that this was the life I deserved to have. We had bought and accepted this knock off version of God's love. We began to make this relationship resemble a marriage. It worked at first. We were happy. Everything seemed to fall into place. Our finances were flowing in abundance. Everything we wanted, we bought. There was no arguing in our house. Compromise was in full operation in our life. The love was still new so everything was perfect. We loved each other with everything in us. I would go to the ends of the earth for him. And he was willing to give up his freedom for our love. Everything was about us. A family was what we were building. Our house was the American dream, a father, a mother, raising children together. We cooked together. We ate dinner together. Dinners were followed by after dinner walks as a family. Beginning love is so exciting and strong. When the love is new, the faith you have in each other is amazing. Everything is right about each other. You are committed to loving what is 'not quite right" about them in the beginning. It was perfect. He could do no wrong. Finally, we had found the right relationship. This love was beautiful. We were beautiful together. And we truly believed that our love would conquer all problems, all worries, and all negativities. In our hearts we knew it was an imitation marriage, but we kept it shining.

Marriage Didn't Come

This trial basis marriage lasted for a year. We were still good, but the relationship slowly began to lose its luster. Our happy days slowly turned into just days. When we moved in together, we only planned for good days. In our future, we only saw sunshine. There was no plan in place for rainy, not so lovable days. We had not prepared for the days when we would not be completely in love with each other. Those days don't exist in 'new' love. In 'new love' everyone is always happy and in love. If anyone had told us we would have days of silence we would not have believed them. But the bad days came. At times, the silence was the only voice being heard.

In the beginning not talking was unthinkable. Now, living in the same house, sometimes talking was unbearable. Living together seemed like the next logically good idea in the beginning. Now the longer we lived together the farther away marriage was moving. The longer we lived together, the more we began to dislike each other. The longer we lived together, the more we didn't want to be married to each other. There were times that we did not want to date each other, or co-parent together. The days of if this relationship would last forever anymore. Our good days were awesome. When we agreed it was like fireworks. But our bad days............. Our bad days were tumultuous. Our disagreements were like bombs. Within months, this knock off version of marriage begin to fall apart. We began arguing about everything. We went from talking all the time to not talking at all. There was a time when all we wanted was each other. Now that was all we didn't want. I remember crying myself to sleep because this relationship was the LAST place I wanted to be. But I could not leave. My boys loved their daddy. He was the first boyfriend I had brought into my oldest son's life. They had formed a father – son bond that would hurt to break up. My son got excited when he came home. He was the first live- in daddy my son had ever had. With this relationship, I had finally given my son a present, full-time father. Making the decision to end the relationship would be like taking his daddy away. I could not do that.

Our super strong love was weaker than we thought. This perfect love was dismantling fast. The only thing that was certain about our relationship was that neither one of us wanted to be in it. But neither one of us wanted to be the one say it failed. And neither one of us wanted to hurt our son. How do you tell a 5-year-old that his perfect family was flawed? How do you tell a kindergartner that their family is breaking up because mommy and daddy don't like each other anymore? We both were courageous enough to brave the ridicule of rushing into this relationship too quickly. But neither one of us had the courage to look a 5-year-old in the face and tell him we were breaking up his world. So, we didn't. We just stayed. We kept pretending. We kept loving each other in the presence of these little eyes. We even had a few almost good times. Our lives went on like that for seven years... loving each other one day, hating each other the next two. Marriage was not even a consideration anymore. We got engaged in 2003. We got married in 2010. During those seven years, we broke up three times. Our daughter was born. He had extra relationships. I acquired new "friends". I felt hurt, pain, and betrayal. I developed trust issues and insecurities. We kept up appearances for family. Our kids were somewhat oblivious to the troubles in our relationship. The love was still there but at this point it was mixed with familiarity. Both of us were over thirty. We were well beyond dating age. And we already knew each other. We selfishly stayed together because we did not want to go through the trouble of learning someone new. Even though our relationship was a disaster, it provided a level of comfort and security in our lives. We knew what we had with each other. Our idea of this perfect relationship had gone out the window. And we now had several reasons to never commit. The driving force behind us lasting so long was selfishness. Both of us trying to outlast each other. Plus, the idea of either of us being happy with someone else was unreal. The one thing that attracted me to my husband was his potential for greatness. I saw greatness in him, and I wanted to be a part of it. And after investing so much of myself in this relationship for seven years, I did not want another woman to come in and reap the benefits of the man he was destined to be. I fought to share his worse. I felt that I was the ONLY woman that deserve to share his best. So, I stayed. It proved to be a huge mistake. I cried many nights. I compromised a lot, even when I was right. I took second to what seemed like everything. I secretly hated him. I did not trust him. I accepted a lot of things from him that were beneath my worth as a woman. I was cheated on. I became content with being the main chick. Don't get me wrong, I was no walk in the park either. I cursed him out. I was mean. I shot down everything he thought about doing. I was anti-social and refuse to engage in his world. I felt abandoned so therefore I isolated myself. And I made sure he felt my isolation. I secretly hated myself for ever loving him. I was cold and unfeeling. He eventually found comfort elsewhere. And I became bitter. While he flexed his manhood, I achieved victim status. I became the loving, faithful girlfriend that didn't deserve this betrayal and pain. There were times when I wanted to be anywhere else. But I had kids. I had invested too much. And I was not a quitter. So, I stayed.

We Got Married

What do you do when wish you could just walk away from the relationship? What do you do when you hate who you are with them? What do you do when the sight of them or their voice makes you want to instantly disappear? I found myself constantly praying and asking God to give you the strength to walk away from him? With all of the turmoil, we made a decision about us. We decided to get married.

Our decision to get married was more about responsibility than love. We had a responsibility to make this family work. The adult thing to do was to put aside ourselves and make it work for the kids. Breaking up was child's play. The "I'm not gonna be your friend anymore' mentality was easy. We were both over thirty. It was time to grow up. And as I stated, I am not a quitter. Neither was he. The one thing we had in common was that we both had to win. We would stay in the relationship as long as it took for the other person to quit. We would play this game to the death. Winning was a must for both of us. So, we got married.

I never believed we would get married. When we got married, I didn't believe it would last. "Why not try it?" I asked myself. We had already been together for seven years. That's a lot of time to give to someone without some sort of return. In the conversation about getting married I said to him, "This marriage just must work. If it doesn't, oh well. I'm done fighting for 'us'. I'm tired. I got no more fight left." And he agreed. In my mind, happiness was never going to happen. I think he felt the same way. Despite the secret wants to be free of each other, we said "I do". I entered the marriage with some serious issues"

I didn't trust him.

I did not like who I was with him.

I had no security in our relationship My heart was closed to him.

I felt like he wanted to be with someone else, anyone else, but me.

He was not the same man I fell in serious like with.

I still felt betrayed.

I felt like I would never be enough for him. AND….

I was no longer committed to the relationship, And on top of it all, I was back to looking for that replica of God's love. I strongly desired that renewed fellowship with God.

Silent treatment, dislike for one another, wanting out, hurt, discord, loss of security, massive disagreements, separations. The solution of marriage seemed logical to us. Marriage can fix all this. All we had to do was bring our relationship back in right standing with God. He would wave his godly wand and presto-Happily Ever After. I decided to marry him with all my baggage. I felt like I could work through them in the marriage. Doing it right, would fix everything. The words 'I do" was the magic that would make everything okay. But it didn't!

Chapter 3 BECOMING ONE

A Beautiful Old Beginning

Marriage at first was blissful. Everything in our relationship felt new again. We felt that living together outside the sanctity of marriage limited our abilities to seek God's help for our troubles. Getting married felt like freedom. No more fornication. No more trying to hide from God. Having sex outside of marriage may not bother everyone, but it bothered us. Being former Christians, we knew what the bible said about premarital sex. It was never okay with us. Marriage lifted that cloud from over us. Now we could pray for our issues. We were finally doing it right. And now God was pleased with our relationship. For a while we were getting along with each other. There was a positive burst in our friendship. We stopped arguing about everything. Our conversation towards each other changed. Teamwork was our new way of interacting with each other. Our problems seemed to have ended. Marriage worked. Getting married seemed to have fixed us. We were progressing in our new life as husband and wife. Life felt like it started over for us. There was so much we knew about each other as boyfriend and girlfriend. But I knew nothing of him as my husband. He had never seen the wife in me. Marriage brings a new level of commitment to the table. This was new. Even sex felt new. We were rediscovering each other in these new life positions. And I think we liked them. Everything was different as a married couple. Your perspective changes when you vow yourself to someone until death. You love different. You share different. You laugh different. Your happy moments mean more. Everything was different. It was a good different. It was intriguing and fascinating. Before the "I dos" we were looking for a way out. We could not stand each other. After we exchanged vows, we loved each other again. We were back to making plans for the future. I began feeling like maybe this thing might just work. We were really trying to make this relationship work. I began to say to myself, "If I use the little fight I had left for this marriage, maybe it could help me get over my issues." So, I began to fight, again. This time I did not fight alone. He joined in. And it was working. We laughed more. Some of the good times came back. Everything in our world seemed to be improving. We thought we were on our way to a real marriage and real happiness. Life was good for a while. We enjoyed being married. We became advocates for giving up fornication and doing it God's way. The honeymoon period lasted for about six months. Then our first disagreement came. We worked together and solved it without an argument. We began talking about everything again. We agreed to be more honest with each other, share our feelings, be more accountable to each other, be more considerate, and listen more. And to some extent we did what we agreed to do. One day we had a small disagreement that turned into a huge argument. In an instant, all of my old issues came flooding back to the surface. The meanness, and hurtful words came back. The profanity, the name calling all came back. Reality came crashing in and we realized that nothing in our relationship had changed.

Marriage had not fixed me or him. We were still two broken people trying to put together a whole marriage. All of the problems were still there. And they seemed to have gotten bigger. We didn't talk to each other for weeks. Our strategy for solving problems was to wait until we were no longer mad then just resume our relationship from that point. We never fixed anything. After the anger subsided, we would decide not to revisit the issue again. We just let it die. This approach seemed to work at first. What we did not realize was that it was making things worse. The arguments got worse. The silent treatments lasted longer. We only broke silence to argue. We were talking, or should I say cursing, at each other. Our relationship resembled the old relationship before the "I Do". The difference was that now we could ask God to fix our new marriage. Because we were no longer fornicating, we could actually ask God for help. We always knew we could pray about us, but we no longer felt like our lifestyle would block our path to God. So we prayed and asked God to fix our marriage. We had not asked God to re-enter our lives just fix this marriage. We were not ready to live for God, we just wanted a better relationship. We were trying to get God to fix the marriage without actually letting him in it. Now. how is God expected to fix a marriage He's not invited into. The next few years of our marriage was a roller coaster. Each smooth ride was followed by a rough one. As time passed, the smooth rides got shorter. We still had issues that had not been resolved. Our issues had been there so long they

had become like family. We were used to them. The issues in our marriage had become our marriage. We did not argue as much. At this point in our marriage, we would just not talk about things. We were not resolving any issues, we just lived around them.
Understand, issues are a part of life and marriage. Everyone has them. Unresolved issues build problems. Problems are NOT a part of life. The bible has no instructions on dealing with problems. It does instruct us on dealing with issues. It instructs us to deal with issues immediately. In my opinion things had gotten better, and worse. We were coexisting. Plans of building on life with an "if" echoing in the background. After some time pass our problems seemed to just disappear. Noticed I used the word "seemed" Not talking about them does not mean they don't exist. Not

talking about your problems only means they are not getting resolved. Constantly avoiding problems puts your relationship in a false sense of reality. You begin to believe that everything is getting better because your problems are no longer allowed to remain on the surface. What we didn't realize was that buried problems are like seeds planted. And deciding not to deal with them is like sunlight and water. Adding the right nourishment: anger, distrust, resentment, silence, the problems began to produce fruit.

The fruit of these unresolved problems manifested itself in every disagreement we had. There would be huge explosions over minor things. Everything became an issue of distrust. I was governed by my pain of being hurt. I lived in the viewpoint of "I was faithful, I don't deserve this." As my boyfriend, he cheated on me. But my husband never cheated on me. The only issue I had as his wife was that I was still being governed by the hurt of being his girlfriend. I threw around the 'divorce' word at the slightest conflict. Everything ended in 'maybe divorce is the best option'. Everything else seemed to work but our relationship. At this point in our marriage arguments became really easy to fix – silent treatment. You can't argue if you are not speaking. We fixed everything but us. After a while, we stopped working on our marriage and focused on keeping our family together. He had changed some in an effort to keep peace. I could see his changes, but I couldn't accept them. He constantly apologized for his mistreatment of me as my boyfriend. He was genuinely sorry for hurting me. But I was still in victim mode. His apologies were not enough compensation for the pain he caused. I trusted him more than anyone else. And he misused that trust. I could not let it go. And I made sure he did not forget how I felt. His past betrayals were my weapons of choice in every argument... his lying... his extra relationships... his walking out. In every situation I was the victim, even when I was wrong. Everything was his fault. If he had not hurt me life would have been different. Oh, I had mastered victim status. Tears were an everyday part of my life. I was a functioning victim. I mastered life with baggage. I got so used to the baggage in my life that it became life. A marriage without happiness seemed obtainable. Don't get me wrong, I love being married. I loved having a husband. But I hated being his wife. There was so much pain between us. It became too much for us to deal with, but I really did want the marriage. I really wanted to fix it. I needed for us to fix it. It's hard to take the next step when you don't know what the next step is. How do we fix this? We never fixed anything. We just quit. There was so much at stake. We were hurting. And our marriage wasn't working. One day we were home alone, and I decided that we could start working on the minor problems in our relationship. I started what should have been a casual, peaceful conversation. I was not proposing that we fix any of the problems, simple build on top of them. The conversation did not go as I planned. I opened the gates, and years' worth of problems came flooding out. Five minutes into the conversation and we were screaming and yelling. All the arguments we did not have, all of the sleepless nights, all of the anger, all of the suppressed tears came back at once. Everything we hadn't said, was said. Two hours later and this time he suggested divorce. He stormed out and I cried. This was not how it played out in my head. We were supposed to decide to work on our marriage, both of us, at the same time. I felt like I had fought by myself for so long. I thought that we were finally in a place where I could enlist him in the fight. I did not know that he was already in a place of quitting. I was in a place where I had just decided to give it one last fight. He was on the edge of divorce. Both of us are stubborn and strong willed. When emotions are high, pride is the only emotion that wins. Neither one of us was willing to admit fault. Neither one of us was willing to take that first step of compromise. Both of our prides had to win.

My pride was not about to let me admit that I wanted the marriage more than anything else. I could admit that I was somewhat at fault for our problems. But my pride was not going to allow me to be vulnerable enough to fight for this relationship alone anymore. He said he wanted a divorce. It didn't matter if he meant it or not, that's what he said. And my pride would allow me to give him THAT even if it was not what my heart wanted.

He returned hours later, still mad. I was still mad too. But I was also hurt. We had broken up many times before but divorce was something totally different. Divorce was the final step. Divorce meant failure. After years of fighting through everything, it was finally going to be over. But I couldn't give up without winning. I am a winner. I have to win.

I, myself, cannot admit failure until I have given my all and it still don't work. And even then, I can't admit failure. I know I had not given my all. So, I proposed that we postpone our decision until we were no longer angry. But he refused. He said that prolonging divorce would just make the situation worse. He said that we just needed to let it go. My hurt turned to rage. In my rage, I agreed to divorce. I asked him to move out and asked him to leave his house key. And He did. We told the kids the next day. Our princess was too young to understand what was going on. My boys cried. It tore them up. My heart crumbled in pieces. My boys never show emotion. Nothing really bothers them. We trained them to brush off everything and move on. They cried!!! Pride has no chance when it comes to the well-being of our children. It was okay when the decision was about just us. But now we were hurting the kids. He proceeded to move out. My boys stuck to my side and refused to talk to him. My baby girl loved her daddy and that's all she knew. For one week he visited. We made the decision to tear the family apart and I was actually watching it happen. I returned to praying. I realized that I was not free. I still had the same issues. And now I had more. Up until now, my issues were always with him. But I had played a part in hurting my kids. My selfishness! My stubbornness! My PRIDE! Now, I had issues with myself. Not only did I have to seek God for help in forgiving him. I needed help forgiving myself. I cried a lot more. I hurt a lot more. Neither one of us could live with the pain we were causing our kids. My oldest son became very protective of me. He automatically took on the responsibility of taking care of me. My husband had raised him to always watch out for me. And he was ready to take on the task of being the man of the house. He was hurting but he was raised to be tough. Our youngest son completely shut down. His conversation with me was scarce. He only talked to me when he needed to. My baby boy always showed his adoration for me. He always wantedto talk to me. He would often come into my room just to check on me. That behavior stopped. He never said he was mad with me, but I knew he was. He stopped talking to his dad all together. Whenever my husband would stop by, my baby boy would go in his room and make himself busy. When he finally talked to me through text, he stated that he thought his dad and i were being childish. He felt like we could make it work if we wanted to. The harsh reality of it all was that he was right. Pride is childish. Being willing to lose everything instead of admitting fault, is childish. Throwing away the whole family unit because you don't want to work on the hard issues of relationship, Is Childish! Truth is, we had not tried, not really.

Children see, know, and understand more than adults think. We allowed the anger to dissipate as usual. And one week later, my husband and I had a talk. We made the decision to give it one more try. This time we would give it our all. Or whatever we had left.

Chapter 4 INVITING GOD IIN

One of the first decisions we made was to go to marriage counseling. Marriage counseling is expensive so we quickly gave that up. I knew that if the marriage had a chance of working, we both had to want it. We wanted it to work but we wanted it to come easy. Just like it fell apart, we wanted it to come back just that easy. Neither one of us was willing to invest anything but a little time. The breakdown in our marriage costed us nothing monetarily. We both agreed that we would not spend all that money on a probability. Divorce was only $409. I wanted to do whatever it took to make this marriage work as long as i did not have to give up anything. Our assumption about counseling was that they would make us talk about our problems. We could talk on our own for free. So we decided that we would just start talking. The only problems with that were that communication was not a strong attribute in our relationship. Life had taught me not to allow people to build relationships with me. I learned not to let people get to close to me. Talking about our problems would require me to open up to him and be honest about how i felt. I was afraid of the hurt that would come out if I opened up. My fear was that I could not handle everything that was wrong with me. If I opened up I would lose control of myself and fall apart. I prided myself on always being in control of my emotions and my world. I believed that it was safer to keep everything built up within myself. But things were spinning out of control, and I was franticly struggling to keep it from unraveling. I felt like the weight of my issues would kill me if I had to face them. I did not feel strong enough to deal with my own emotions. I had avoided dealing with our problems because I was too afraid to let anyone into my heart. I wanted to be happy but was afraid of the process it would take to build happiness. So, I fought with myself. I dealt with myself by not really dealing with the problems within myself. I prayed and asked God to help me but was too afraid to let Him in. The more God tried to heal my heart, the more I fought against change. One thing I learned about God is that he is a gentleman and he's patient. He patiently waited until I was tired of fighting against change. The weight of being me got to be so much that it overpowered the fear of letting God in, I just wanted to be free. I needed to be free. And I was now willing to do whatever it took to get free. We made an attempt to talk about our feelings. it didn't go so well. Talking about our feelings left us feeling too vulnerable. Vulnerability in our eyes was a sign of weakness. He and I were both strong minded individuals. Neither one of us was going to show any signs of vulnerability in front of the other. Previous attempts at talking about our feelings always ended in accusations and anger. Deep down, we both wanted everything just to work out. We wanted a change in our relationship without either one of us actually having to change. In my eyes, I did not need changing. His perspective was the same about himself. So we decided to put all of our energy into working solely on our relationship. My rationale was that I had to put my all into this last effort. If it worked out, then we all win. If it didn't, then at least I could walk away with no regrets. The lessons I learned would either make this marriage better or make my next one great. To us, inviting God in simply meant going back to church. We decided to find a church home. After a few church services I began to long for my fellowship with God. I had not been to church in twelve years. Asking God for anything felt awkward to me. I had lived the way I wanted for all this time. I had not required or asked for God's help for twelve years. Church felt strange. There was such a disconnect between me and God. I was out of place at church. Part of the reason church was so awkward was because i knew I was approaching God selfishly. I was not interested in what God wanted out of this deal. I had my hand out expecting God to do everything for me. God is not Santa clause.

He isn't there to just give to you. With every gift comes an expectation. I am in church, spiritually standing with my arm stretching as far as it could go, careful, not to get to close to God, asking him to do something for me. I was not used to this type of relationship with God. When your life is in right standing with God you feel like you can ask for anything. I remember having the confidence to go to God about anything. But because I had lived contrary to His word for so long, I felt like i was admitting defeat. It's like having to ask for something from a person you know you did wrong. I did not like how being in church made me feel. I have always been successful at everything I did. but sitting in church, I felt like a failure. Because my husband story is similar to mine in that we were both backsliders, I thought he felt the same way.

To my surprise he seemed right at home in church. He jumped right back into worship service like he had never left. We became committed to finding a permanent church home. To our kids, going to church regularly was strange as well. They were receptive to the idea of going to church if that meant we were not getting a divorce. We began to attend church faithfully. We were desperate for God to fix this marriage. Our agreement was to let God in our relationship enough to fix the relationship, not us. If we did not get Jesus in this marriage, there would be no marriage. We visited several churches. I will admit, it did help a little. But the change in our marriage was insignificant. We still argued. The tension of our relationship was still very strong. I still had all of my issues with him. He still had all of his issues with me. We had not asked God to enter our marriage. We had not repented for our sins. Neither one of us wanted to live a Christian lifestyle. We just wanted God to fix the relationship. Because there seemed to be little improvement in our relationship, we revisited the idea of marriage counseling. He inquired of the senior pastor of Light of Life Worship Center church. And I talked to the first lady. She gave me some very real advice. She said that although I needed to be in church and should invite God into my marriage, solely attending church wouldn't fix my marriage. In order for us to save this marriage, we would have to change. Us change? That was not the answer I was looking for. So, we stop going to church . Now how are we going to fix this marriage if we didn't go to church? I knew we were two broken people. I knew that the only way we would fix our marriage was to fix ourselves. After playing the victim for so long, I wanted to be fixed. I cried daily. I had so many issues in myself. I often wished I could just run away from being me. I felt trapped in my life. I wanted to be free. I didn't like myself and I wanted out. I began praying for just myself. I decided that this marriage was going to end however it was going to end. That was no longer my concern. How was I going to deal with myself when it was over. My life was about being a wife and mother. Outside of my family role, who was I? Outside of the pain and hurt, who was the real me? There was so much buried in me that it became the new me. But I no longer wanted to be the new me. The new me was miserable. She was unforgiving and cold. The woman I had become was not happy at all. She didn't love herself or life. I hated being her. I remember laughing and being happy. I wanted my laughter back. I wanted my peace back. I longed for happier days. I slowly came to the realization that it was time for me to finally deal with myself and my issues. The hard truth was that most of my issues had nothing to do with my husband. I was the problem. Truth is, I had most of these issues before I met my husband. I was so good at shutting down that I forgot about all these unresolved issues. I quickly realized that going into shut down mode does not make the issues go away. One day you are going to have to deal with all those issues. And the longer you take, the more issues you have to face. My time had come. So, I got real selfish. I stop praying for my marriage and my husband. I stopped asking God to fix this marriage. My prayers shifted from 'us' to 'me'. My prayer became "God fix me!" If God had answered my first prayer and gave me the perfect marriage, I would have messed it up. There were so many things wrong with me. Before God could work on our marriage, he had to work on us. We had to want to be fixed individually. I decided to ask God to work on me. Wholeness is a personal desire. Wanting to be fixed is something you must want for yourself. My only prayer was "Lord, fix me." I didn't ask God to fix him. I didn't pray that God change him. I selfishly decided to let him deal with himself.

Chapter 5: BECOMING THE WIFE GOD HAD IN MIND

Learning to Be Quiet!!

The first thing i did was repent for my sins. I was brutally honest with God. I needed to first get atonement. I asked God's forgiveness for everything I knew was wrong about me. I was angry, spiteful and vengeful. And I was very mean. Then I started dealing with the issues I know I had. I lack trust. I had commitment issues. I did not like myself. I had become a victim. This was not a five-minute repentance session. When you have as many issues as i had, you need to spend some time apologizing to God. The more i apologized, the more my ugly behavior became noticeable. I repented a lot. I ended every prayer with "Lord fix me."

When I got mad, sad, or withdrawn... "Lord fix me." I had so much pain, so many disappointments... "Lord fix me." I'm mean and hateful at times, "Lord fix me." I was so tired of being this way. All I wanted was to be happy. All I wanted was peace. I just wanted to be free. "Lord fix me."

I went pleading to God defeated and crying, "Lord please fix me. I'm tired. God I can't do this anymore. Please FIX ME!" And He did. The first change God made in me was to shut my mouth. He taught me to listen. Listening was extremely hard for me because I came from a long line of strong minded, opinionated women. Coincidentally most of those strong minded, opinionated women are also divorced or have never been married. Allow me to pause to give you a little advice, be mindful who you fashion yourselves after because their methods will yield their results. If you do not want their outcome, don't follow their example. I did not want the result of divorce. I wanted my marriage to last.

Being silent taught me how to listen. As I began to listen, I began to hear all the things I was doing to my husband. I began to hear what he needed in a wife. I began to hear his pain in dealing with me. As God was working on me, I began to see my fault in my marriage. One of the hardest things I ever had to do was to admit that I played a role in this bad marriage. I was the perfect wife. I had high standards. I was dedicated. Loyalty was my strongest attribute. Thoughtful, loving, supportive, I was all that. He should have been nominating me for WIFE OF THE

YEAR. In my mind, this was the wife my husband had. Mr. Bush told a different story. His wife was very judgmental and selfish. She never cheated but she never let him forget that he did. The woman he was married to was very anti-social and only supported the things she cared about. His image of his wife was nothing like the image I had of his wife. The attributes that I thought I was portraying was not being perceived or received that way. I always had his best interest at heart. But that came across as bossy and overbearing. I put his needs before my own. I put his happiness before mine and got mad when he did not make the same choice concerning me. That angry made me controlling and possessive. The woman my husband was married to was mean and self-righteous. She walked around acting like she was perfect. And according to him she was strong willed and uncompromising. Those were never the attributes I wanted to portray. I realized that I was asking for more than I was giving. I wanted him to see the wife I was trying to be. He had some changing to do too but this process was about me. I came across a Facebook post that said, 'Be the change you want to see." I prayed, "Lord, make me the wife you want me to be." I never prayed that he made me the wife my husband wanted. I figured if I became the wife God wanted me to be then I would be the wife my husband wanted. Or I would be a great wife for my next husband. Selfishly I was still praying for my own agenda in this marriage. But God had other plans. All God needed was for me to be willing to change. Now I was willing, unaware of the enormous changes He had planned for me. I began to do the things my husband needed me to do, without keeping score. At the beginning of every situation in life you are given the opportunity to do the right thing, and the wrong thing. It is not always easy to do the right thing. You will not always see the immediate results of choosing to do the right thing. My decision to be the wife my husband needs was an 'in spite of" decision. It was also a decision that I made within myself, independent of him. I did not tell him that I had decided to be a better wife. And it was not easy. The funny thing about my decision was that in the back of my mind I was expecting him to also make the decision to change. He did not. I also made the decision to change expecting God to simultaneously spark a need to change in him. But it was not his time yet. It is easier to see a person's fault rather than to see the good in them. I was not in a place to accept a change in him without being suspicious. I was still too judgmental, too un-trusting, and too self-righteous. I only had the willingness to change. I had not changed yet. I had just begun the process of transformation. The old me was still in operation. But the change God began making in me was amazing. God began to make me a nicer, more loving person. God dealt hugely with my anger and attitude. I was constantly asked to step out of my normal ways and do things differently. I learned to speak my heart without accusation and anger.

Another hard lesson in was taught was to walk away angry and come back calm and compromising. No matter how mad I got, I could not react the way I wanted to. I began to see that my actions had reactionary effects on my relationships. Some of the reactions I got from my husband was in response to what I had done to him. After months of allowing God to fix me, I could feel the changes in myself. But my husband could not see the changes in his wife. I was still a work in progress. I had to learn to adjust to the new me, work the new me, love the new me. And then I had to learn to work the new me as his wife, as his partner, as the mother of his kids, as his help meet, and as his example. God had not begun to change him. I still was not praying for him. And i don't know if he was seeking God for himself. I don't think we could have gone through this transformation together. I think if he was going through the same process I was, at

the same time, it would have killed the

process in the both of us. God had to change who I was first. Only God's version of his wife would be able to accept God's version of her husband. When I used to pray for him, I would pray that God make him a better husband. Now I realized that he deserved a better wife. He needed a better wife. I repented for not being the wife he needed. I asked forgiveness for all of my selfishness and betrayal of this marriage. Finally getting over myself, I prayed, "Lord make me the wife he need

The second change God made in me was an increase in my prayer life. I never talked or prayed about my feelings. I was always afraid of opening the flood gates. I knew I had bottled up issues. But I had lost count of how many. I felt like I had too many issues for me to handle so i didn't deal with any of them. I stayed trapped in this state of my life because it was familiar. My life had begun to crumble, and I felt powerless to stop it. And I was tired. I was tired of being stuck. I was tired of crying. I was tired of not being understood. I was tired of arguing, fussing, and fighting. So, I talked to the only person I trusted with my feelings, God. I prayed a lot, about everything. We were still having difficult times. But after every situation, instead of crying, I prayed. 'Lord help me to be more understanding, less judgmental, and more loving." The more intense our "situations" were, the more I prayed. If I got angry at him, I prayed. When he did something that reminded me of past pain, I prayed. I prayed so much during this transformation, I developed a constant prayer life. With every prayer, God was penetrating another layer of issues in my heart. Without realizing it, I was releasing the very things that I was afraid of letting go. With every prayer, God took away something and gave me peace. The burden of being me was lifting and I did not even know it. The very process that I thought would kill me was making me stronger. I felt a smile developing on the inside of me. Sometimes we don't know the weight of our issues until they are being lifted. I did not realize how heavy of a burden I was carrying. Suddenly, my life seemed livable again.

Give Myself Away

We attended church faithfully for a while. Our marriage remained the same. So, we stopped going as a family. Divorce was no longer an option but 'til death do us part was still not realistic either. I became miserable with my life again. The crying eventually came back. But to my surprise, so did the praying. Then finally I had had enough of being 'not happy". I rededicated my life to Christ for the last time. I didn't tell my husband. My relationship with Jesus was a personal one. I wanted him to make the same decision. We had talked about rededicating our lives to Christ. Both with Christian backgrounds, we both missed the presence of God in our lives. Together, we made a unanimous decision that we needed God in our marriage. I felt the overwhelming need for a relationship with God, I thought he did too. He seemed to really enjoy the church we were attending. But he still made excuses. He still was not sure if he wanted to live a

Godly life. The day I accepted the love of God, stepped into the aisle, and took that faith walk to the altar, was the day my husband decided not to rededicate his life to Christ. He decided to run in the opposite direction. Up until that very moment we did everything together. We shared in each other's decisions. If one of us decided we wanted to try something, the other one would try it too. If we both did not like it, then neither one of us continued doing it. Salvation was the first thing we could not and did not do together. I did it alone. I had his support. he always supported me in anything I decided to do. But he did not partner with me in this decision. I would have to fly solo on this next journey in my life. M y husband wanted no part of this decision. Normally if I make a good decision, my husband would jump on board with it.

This time he did not. And the longer it took him, the more i doubted. Because he did not join in the decision, I struggled with sticking to it. In my heart i kept second guessing whether or not is was a good decision. I was uncommitted to this new life for months. I fought against myself. I wanted this so bad for myself, and for us. But he wanted no part in it. It seemed like every step I took towards salvation; my husband took two steps back. After all the struggles, the best decision in my life, looked like it could be the worst decision for our marriage. My heart was truly heavy because I really did want my marriage. Many times, I said to myself that either God was transforming me in to the wife he needs or he is preparing me for my next husband. That was the hurt and disappointment talking. Truth is, I did not want a next husband. I wanted this husband. I really did love this man. I loved him so much that I considered giving up salvation to keep him. But my desperate need to finally be free won over all in the end. I remember the day I decided that if I had to, I would be saved by myself. It was a Saturday night. I walked in our bedroom and asked my husband if he was going to church the next morning. He said no. In his mind, if he showed no interest in it, I would lose interest. I hesitated, Then I replied, "Well, just drop me off." Then I turned and walked out of the room. I walked in a new freedom at that moment. He just looked at me. After getting my clothes ready for church, I set my alarm and went to sleep. The real test came the next morning. When the alarm went off, he did not move. To his surprise, I did. I got up, got dressed all the while letting him lay there. I just knew in the back of my mind that if he saw me getting dressed, he would change his mind. He didn't. He figured if he laid there until it was time to go, I would change my mind. I didn't. I woke him up and asked him to drop me off. I did not drive at the time, so he had to take me. And he did. When we got to the church, I kissed him and got out of the car. The walk to the door was the longest walk I had ever taken. I fought with the idea of changing my mind and going back home with my husband. But I made it. I went in alone. Sat down alone. And praised God, alone. I had a little talk with Jesus that morning and promised God that I would live for him BY MY SELF, if I have to. Church service was awesome. For the first time in months, I made a decision that made me feel good. I was proud of myself for sticking to my decision to live for Christ. I went up to the alter for prayer and then Minister whispered in my ear, "God says trust Him. He is concerned about everything that concerns you." So, my journey began.

God slowly changed the way I responded to life. The nights I would have spent crying, I spent praising God. I was nicer to my husband. I was nicer to everyone. God was transforming all of my relationships. I started listening to gospel music at home. I would put on my headphones, sit in the corner of our bed and sing praises to God. When I praised God, my husband would walk out of the room and let me have my moment. He was watching even though he wasn't speaking on it. But I could see that he was beginning to believe that I was serious about my life with Christ.

It was about a month into my transformation that God really began to make me the wife he needed. I began attending church regularly, to my surprise, my husband and kids came with me. My husband was still dead set against giving his life to Christ. But the difference God was making in me, was intriguing to him. I began apologizing to him for my part in the breakdown of my marriage. I began to realize that some of my problems in my marriage started before him. Our problems were becoming issues again. He still had not committed to God, so we still had friction. The hurt was still there. And I still had trust issues. The pivotal moment in my faith was when it came time to let my guard down and give my husband access to my heart again. This was the last obstacle I had to cross. Everything in me wanted to trust God. And at the same time, everything in my past proved that this was a bad idea. My husband had hurt me too many time. He had walked out to many times. I realized that all of the problems in our relationship was not his fault. I also realized that all of my issues were not his doing. But a lot of them were. He had begun to make changes within him as well. I could see he was different. But he still had a lot to change. I was not perfect, but I had changed a lot. He had not even met me halfway. Everything in me reminded me that he was not worthy of my heart again. I wrestled with this last step for weeks. It did not help that my husband was being the same him that i had all these issues with. God was

telling me to trust this man. He had done nothing to prove that he was worth my trusting him again. He had not tried to change or be anything i told him i needed from him. Trusting him again would be like opening myself up to more pain and disappointment. Surely, God was not asking me to do that. Refusing not to trust my husband was also refusing not to trust God. But i did trust God. God was the only one i trusted. Refusing not to trust my husband also meant going back to the old me.
And I did not want to be her again. She was miserable. So I decided to try this trust thing. The decision was easier than the process. I remember the day I finally let go. I was sitting in church at The Light Center. The worship service was soo powerful that I began to cry. I had cried so much in church over the

past weeks. This particular Sunday the tears kept flowing. I cried through the worship service, through the welcome service, through the bible reading, and through the preached word. I remember looking at my husband and saying to God," I can't. I can't give him my heart again. I can't trust him with me. I can't go through that pain again. What if I don't make it through this time? I want to trust you God, but I can't." I cried through my whole conversation with God. I cried because all I wanted was to be free. Free from the hurt! Free from the anger! Free to trust! Free to love! I was tired of leaving the house of God with the same burdens I came with. But what God was asking me to do was bigger than the new me. I had forgiven, but had not forgotten. I trusted God with my emotions, but not with me. History has taught me not to trust ANYONE with me. Not God and definitely not my husband. But that would mean walking out of God's house with the same burdens i walked in with again. I did not want to do that either. I had fought through too much to be free. I'm too close to turn back now. I sat there crying and negotiating with God. I said to God, "I tell you what I'll do. I'll give YOU my heart. And when he is ready, if he gets ready, you can give it back to him." I felt a release in my body as if God had accepted my terms. And I released everything to God that day. As I sat there, tears flowing, God was taking away all of the hurt, the anger, the distrust, the disappointment... Everything! I did not go to the altar that day for prayer. God met me at my seat. The tears were still flowing when I walked around to give my offering. GOD

TOOK IT ALL! When I left church that Sunday, I felt like I could fly.

The life that followed that Sunday was bright. I stop being angry at the simplest things. I began to see the wife he really had. She was horrible. I no longer wanted to be her. I felt different. I wanted to be different. I welcomed the transformation. For the first time, in the history of your marriage, I felt like it had a chance. I did not care if he gave his life back to Christ or not. I loved this man. With all of the pain and anger gone, I was now free to love. It was okay to love. All the walls fell down. I opened my heart and welcomed the healing. I was loving the new me. And so was he. I was not as mean. I still had some issues. But I was not judgmental. I was in a place where I could really hear his pains and hurts. I could apologize and mean it. I could talk about things without accusing. I no longer blamed him for the relationship issues that I brought into the relationship. And I no longer expected him to fix me. I was in a good place. Instantly my marriage was in a better place. I reached for peace in every situation. I began to work with him in everything instead of fighting him on everything. I began to really see his heart. And he began to really understand mine. We talked a lot. I stopped crying. I fought through feelings of insecurity and distrust. I began to make mental notes of the things he did differently. I began being kinder to him. God's love for him was taking over me. Patience and understanding became an operational part of me. Pride took a backseat to compromise and unity. I stop doing things for him out of obligation. I just allowed my love to govern my actions. It proved it proved to be challenging at times, but the reward was greater. We smiled more. We began talking in solution tense. I was learning to love him again. And he was learning to love me. As time when on, we spent less time apologizing and more time rebuilding. Long nights of arguing and silent treatments were replaced with long nights of communicating and love making.

We talked about everything. The softer I became towards him, the more he opened up to me. One night we were talking and I was sharing my feelings with him. When it was his turn to share, he clammed up. I started to get upset. I felt like he should be comfortable enough to open up about his innermost feelings. But because we had come so fair with our communication, I feared he would turn back to the way we used to be. I kissed his head and said, " One day, maybe not today, you are going to learn to trust me with your feelings." I reassured him that I loved him and went to sleep. That night I prayed, "God I want to be home to him." I want to be a place where he can be free to be him. I prayed and asked God to make me a place where he don't have to be superman all the time.. where he can let his vulnerabilities show without fear of judgment. I wanted to be his safe place, his familiar place, and his place of rest. When you pray for something, be ready to demonstrate the desire for it immediately. The very next night he opened up. And what poured out was more than I had anticipated. I realized that there was so much i did not know about my husband. We lived together for 12 years. I was certain that i knew the whole him. I never knew his pain. I had no knowledge of his real fears. For twelve years he never felt safe enough to tell me what kept him up nights. He never felt secure enough to let me see him cry or experience the pains of his life. I shared most of my feelings with him. He knew the source of my tears. But as his wife, i knew none of his. That night, he allowed himself a moment of vulnerability. He took a risk. And for the first time in our relationship. I listened. As i listened, I began to understand the human side of my superman. He began to allow me to see the vulnerable side of him. And to his surprise I was receptive and supportive to it. In my transformation, God taught me the importance of being attentive to my reactions with him.

I remember telling him that I never felt his strength as much as I did during that vulnerable moment. The next couple of nights he shared a little more. There were some tears, some laughs, and some prayer. This sparked the start of a beautiful, refreshing level of communication. Two people that hated to talk about their feelings, now talked about everything. Our biggest personal weaknesses became the strength of our relationship. The change God made in his wife brought about even greater changes in my husband. We did not ride off into the sunset or live happily ever after. Our life did not become perfect. But we began to see the perfection in our imperfect love. It started with me saying YES to God's plan for me. He rededicated his life to Christ. He took ownership of his role as lord of our home. The process of transformation began to take place in his life. Because I allowed God to make me the wife he needed, I could easily accept the coming of the husband I needed. I was now in a place where i could accept the changes in him without question. And I became Home, to him. Like with all marriages, there is still friction at times. But now our issues don't last long enough to become problems. God DID That!!! My husband became my best friend, my lover, my confidant, and my ministry partner. When God says trust in him, do it. Believe me, his plans will exceed your every expectation. One year after our decision to get a divorce, we are praising, praying, worshiping, living for, and seeking God TOGETHER. My testimony is simply this: My willingness to trust God and allow him to fix me, awakened a desire in my husband for God to fix him. The result was God teaching us how to fix us. He changed our love and made us one. We gave God a broken relationship. And He helped us Win Our Marriage Back.

Amos 3:3 Can two walk together EXCEPT they be agreed.

Epilogue

I am not a marriage or relationship counselor. This book was written to give insight on the problems and solutions in my marriage. Every marriage is custom made. Each marriage has its own set of unique problems. There are no universal solutions to marital issues. What I learned in my marriage is that communication is key. Communication involves relaying a message and ensuring that it is interpreted in the context that you are sending it. If the other party does not understand your intent, then the message is lost. In my marriage I thought I was being the perfect wife. The intent of my actions were to be supportive, and protective. I was trying to prevent issues from becoming problems. My husband received my actions as overbearing and controlling. I did a lot of things for him, but I kept score. I reviewed the play book every time I did not get my way. That's not communication. I learned not to mother my husband. No adult wants to be parented in their relationship with their spouse. Adults do not like to be told what to do, or what is good for them. My husband didn't. I also learned that loving each other requires a mutual respect for each other. Respect, not just for the person but also for their feelings, thoughts, and ideas. You were not raised in the same house, therefore you will have different views on a lot of things. Both views are right in its own perspective. The objective is to decide which view will be the best practice for your situation. There were a lot of things we did differently. Sometimes my way seemed more logical. Sometimes his way won. We both had great reasons why our learned ways made more sense. The other person's way seemed strange because it was not what we were used to. We agreed to try the other way first before we decided that it would not work. If we could not agree on which way was better, we simply made up our own. OUR WAY became the new best practice for our home.

The importance of God in our relationship was the greatest lesson we learned. Marriage requires constant work. Learning to bring two different backgrounds, upbringings, and perspectives together harmoniously is not a task for the faint at heart. You need a power greater than you human understanding. God is that power. With God's wisdom and guidance, you can learn what to do, what not to do, what to say, and what not to say. If you have a relationship with God, He can give insight on the other person that will help you understand them better. That same godly insight can prevent an issue from forming. God also gives you the grace to forgive and hope. Our personal relationship with God gives us the strength to reach for resolution rather than focus on the problem. Because God's love is active in our lives, our love towards each other is more genuine. We pray together. We worship together. We share in God's love together. Communication between us is easier because of our constant communication with God. He teaches us how to interact with each other. Inviting God back into our lives was one of the best decisions we ever made. Allowing God's love to consume our marriage was the other one. There are no loses in our relationship only wins. Successful marriages are God's original plan. If you learn to trust in His plan, He will navigate you through the rough patches of marriage. The hiccups in your relationship was intended to make you closer and stronger. The saying is true, what does not kill you really does make you stronger. The ultimate goal is to make sure it does not make you bitter. God's presence in operation throughout your marriage will ensure that your love will grow. Now with every situation we grow, Stronger! Wiser! Better! And More In Love with each other

Follow Us on Social Media
Facebook & Youtube:
@Playbook Relationships

Services
**Premarital Counseling/
Wedding Officiant Services**
In select counties in Florida

Relationship Coaching

Contact Us
Phone: 954-451-0879
Email: playbookrelationships@gmail.com

Prayer for Marriage

Father God,

This marriage is a gift that you have entrusted us with. A precious tool that you have given us to build up your kingdom. Together, you have given us the power to conquer our worlds. Thank you for your confidence in us. Thank you for allowing us to be examples of your love, your forgiveness, your mercy, and tender grace in this union

We declare, This Day, that we are one. We will act as one. We will live as one. And be in peace as one. Division no longer lives in our camp. IN EVERYTHING - United We Stand , Back to back, Hand in hand , Leaning on each other, Supporting each other, comforting each other, fighting for each other, and accepting nothing less than absolute victory FOR EACH OTHER.

Looking unto you, the author and finisher of our faith. In Jesus Name, Amen

Wife's Prayer

Father God,

I come to you on behalf of all husbands, my husband in particular. God, I often add to the pressures of society by expecting my husbands to be what the world says I should have in a husband. I apologize. I apologize for adding to the weight of the responsibility that you have given him. I apologize for not being sympathetic to his human limitations and not offering my services as a help to him. I apologize for not allowing him to lean on me. With the extra weight I add, he still manages to stand. - Thank You. Thank You for giving him the strength to stand up to the expectations of him. Thank you for his patience and endurance when dealing with my demands that defy his human capabilities. Thank you that he still manages to get the job done. Thank you for giving him the strength to be my Superman. Help me be a source of strength to him rather than a depletion of might.

Help me to hold him up and cover him with love. God my prayer for my husband is simply this. "Help ME be a help to HIM!!!" In Jesus Name, AMEN.

Husband's Prayer

Father God,

I can do everything imaginable for my wife and it still wouldn't be enough to show her how much she means to me. She is my rock. Like most wives, she constantly works her magic behind the scenes and often without recognition. Well today, I you for thank her. Thank you for her attention to detail. How she will not settle for anything less than the best for me. Thank you for her strength to carry the weight of this family. Thank you for her unyielding love for me. Looking into her eyes is like looking into your purpose for me. Help me be her protector, shield, and comfort. Help me to strengthen her through love and commitment.

Teach me to be the husband she needs, her

partner, her best friend, her wall. God, i want to forever be her king. Allow my love to be her reflection. In Jesus Name, AMEN

www.ingramcontent.com/pod-product-compliance
Lightning Source LLC
Chambersburg PA
CBHW022108160426
43198CB00008B/395